[E.D.'M.A.]

Shivitti: A Review of Ka-Tzetnik 135633's Vision

Didaskalos

Ew Publishing
Bryan W. Brickner

[E.D'M.A.]

Shivitti: A Review of Ka-Tzetnik 135633's Vision

SHIVITTI
(the reminder of the presence of God): A Vision
Ka-Tzetnik 135633

Hebrew Publication
Hakibbutz Hameuchad 1987

First US Publication
Harper & Row 1989

First Gateways Edition 1998

Ew Publishing
Bryan W. Brickner

ISBN: 1507501749

Made in the United States.

Table of Contents

For Zizi ...

By way of a preface

KZ's healing vision of Auschwitz survival, through the use of LSD, is grace-based. This book review offers six gates that attest to Shivitti as the best book of the 20th century; no other book captures and conveys the human, all too human nature of that century.

Bryan W. Brickner
January 2015
Chicago

GATE 1

"Ein braver Kerl!"

Set: *to fix as a distinguishing imprint, sign, or appearance*

> *"Rabbi, why?"*
> *"Because it was so decreed."*
> *"Rabbi, who decreed? Who decreed, Rabbi?"*
> *"Ask God."*[1]

The year is 1976 and KZ is in Dr. Jan C. Bastiaans' office, nervous, and horizontal on a couch. The doctor has a syringe and needle prepared with *lysergic acid diethylamide (LSD)*, and an audio tape recorder ready; KZ will use these tapes to construct his book, *Shivitti (the reminder of the*

---

[1] Shivitti: 10.

presence of God): A Vision Ka-Tzetnik 135633, more than ten years later.

After a few calming words from the doctor, KZ is given the medicine (LSD) and the session begins, the LSD instantly modulating his serotonin system and its 15 receptors. He feels the change – his serotonin system going fully active – and then suddenly, in his mindscape, he's a child again in Rabbi Shilev's classroom. There is great Light: then great Darkness.

Soon he and the Rabbi are boarding the truck that will take them to Auschwitz's crematorium. While boarding, now under full (macro) modulation of his serotonin receptors via LSD, KZ sees skyward *shivitti*; this is a traditional Old Testament verse, Psalm 16:8: "I have set the Lord always before me."

The shivitti is a sign in the therapy (LSD) session for him; it had meaning for KZ and became a guiding sign for him during his five sessions. This is a well-documented serotonin experience; the use of familiar signs to show ourselves to ourselves; LSD sessions don't tell one much … they show one.

The biblical Abraham would also be an example of a serotonin experience; he saw a fire, approached looking for an ember, and heard … the Creative Voice let's say. A Hindu, for another example, would see, feel and hear signs familiar to their mind and world ~ and a Creative Voice as well.

Setting: *the place and conditions in which something happens or exists*

KZ remembers the German S.S. officer overseeing their departure for the crematorium; this time (he didn't before) he sees the German yawn.

This yawn becomes a metaphor, and not just for the boredom of death at Auschwitz; for KZ it signifies indifference to world, to Other, what Hannah Arendt termed thoughtlessness. The German soldier doesn't hate KZ – he doesn't even know him – and yet the German yawningly sees him off to the fire.

The trucking to the crematorium commences, passing through the Auschwitz gate and beneath its infamous phrase: *Arbeit Macht Frei (Work Sets One Free).*

KZ, this time, sees that the shivitti remained aglow in the sky.

Science: *knowledge about or study of the natural world based on facts learned through experiments and observation*

KZ climbs into the truck's coalbin to escape death and the crematorium; Rabbi Shilev and the Others were turned into Auschwitz ash.

KZ hides in the coalbin and truck garage until morning. The driver arrives and is spooked; he runs away and returns with a German S.S. Commander. The officer demands to know who is in the garage or he'll shoot: "I'm a human being!" is KZ's response. He hears the German say: *"Ein braver Kerl!"* *(A tough Chap!)*

At this point, Dr. Bastiaans brings KZ back to 1976 and his current state of being ~ yet in his mind's reality moments from the Auschwitz S.S. Commander. To bring him back, the doctor simply touched KZ; via touch, his Auschwitz mindscape ceased, he suddenly returns (in his being) to the doctor's office and three decades from the S.S. officer's hand, the hand of death.

GATE 2

"Kan nicht lopen."

Set: *to fix as a distinguishing imprint, sign, or appearance*

KZ takes some time to process his vision. Dr. Bastiaans' therapy was patient-centered: patients would make the appointment and schedule their LSD session. KZ notes his nervous confidence:

"My first experience had taught me that before the LSD took over my mind, I had the power to program the direction I wanted the session to take me."[2]

Prior to the injection, Dr. Bastiaans asks KZ about the beach incident; KZ was enjoying some time at the

---

[2] Ibid, 32.

beach when a German tourist innocently admired his branded arm and its number, 135633, as a unique tattoo.

KZ doesn't want to discuss the beach incident; the doctor suggests (urges even) it is the time to look at it; they begin the session.

Setting: *the place and conditions in which something happens or exists*

His serotonin/LSD mind takes him back to a specific day in Auschwitz; he's witness to the burning alive of Gypsy women and children.

KZ is by the pit the Gypsies are in awaiting death; a German S.S. officer tells another Jew to pour kerosene on the women and children. The Dutch Jew, as KZ calls him, exclaimed to the German: *"No! No!!"*

The German kicked the Dutch Jew into the pit (he was able to climb out) and poured the kerosene on the Gypsy women and children himself.

It's not the death horror that KZ recalls in the LSD session; it's the tone and humanness of the Dutch Jew's words that touch him; he'd never heard a Jew speak like that to a German, let alone an Auschwitz Jew to a German S.S.

Science: *knowledge about or study of the natural world based on facts learned through experiments and observation*

The Dutch Jew fell into line with KZ as they shuffled-off and mumbled: *"Kan nicht lopen ... Kan nicht lopen."* KZ understood the man next to him without knowing any Dutch: not being able to walk meant death at Auschwitz.

KZ also tells of another Dutch Jew named "Baby." Baby dies one of those horrible Auschwitz deaths that KZ describes with meaning ~

part of the healing possible in LSD-serotonin system therapy.

After the session, KZ is walking the streets of Leiden, a Dutch city. While walking, the phrase *"Kan nicht lopen"* runs through his mind. He starts to say the words to the passing Dutch. They are confused and try to help yet all he wants to do is say the words. He's in Leiden yet Auschwitz – and he's healing; he's crying and that's a good thing. It's one of the post-effects of LSD, as emotions resurface in usefully healing ways. Tears of sorrowful joy they might be called ... and it's okay to weep.

GATE 3

"Enter the coalbin ..."

Set: *to fix as a distinguishing imprint, sign, or appearance*

KZ re-encounters the story of Jacob's ladder in his third LSD-serotonin session; it was a lesson the Rabbi of Shilev had taught him when he was four.

Now, strengthened by time, the doctor and two LSD-serotonin therapy sessions, KZ is able to recall and experience his question, Jacob's dilemma:

"Did Jacob wrestle with himself? And like me, didn't he know his own name? Is the fear that struck Jacob wrestling

with himself the same fear that strikes me, seeing myself in that S.S. cap?"[3]

KZ sees himself climbing into the coalbin and his rabbi turning away to be ashed by the Auschwitz furnace; skyward is his Jacob's ladder moment: KZ sees his face wearing the S.S. cap and swarmed with vipers, and begs his soul for an answer.

Setting: *the place and conditions in which something happens or exists*

Dr. Bastiaans touches KZ and pulls him away from the Unknown: this is the warning part of the book review and also the medical part.

Taking LSD intravenously is nothing I've experienced or had even heard of before this book. KZ provides a clear warning about using such therapy: an expert guide.

---

[3] Ibid, 64.

KZ also details a thoughtful conversation he had with Dr. Bastiaans on the lack of him using his name (Mr. De-Nur) to write his books: KZ writes using the author name of Ka-Tzetnik 135633.

Mr. De-Nur recognizes this defensive wall he constructs by speaking in the third-person; with the LSD-serotonin therapy his "I" and "me" show up.

Science: *knowledge about or study of the natural world based on facts learned through experiments and observation*

Professor Bastiaans and Mr. De-Nur have a long conversation while sitting outdoors. KZ is in a campus park enjoying the day and Bastiaans wanders-up and sits with him. They talk as colleagues and friends not like patient and doctor. Bastiaans tells KZ that he read his books after their first session and was struck by the coalbin; he suggested (to paraphrase) that he may still be in there, or that he left part of himself in there. Bastiaans says to KZ: "If you enter this coalbin, the womb of your rebirth, as into your soul, you'll find the answers waiting."

KZ: "I suddenly thought, *'Enter the coalbin as into my own soul.'* Then I am also the coalbin."[4]

---

[4] Ibid, 69.

GATE 4

"Nicht Juden austreten!!!"

Set: *to fix as a distinguishing imprint, sign, or appearance*

KZ recalls the first time he heard "Hitler's warriors" at the beginning of the fourth LSD-serotonin session. It's early September 1939, and Germany has just invaded Poland. His village is one of the first hit and the German soldiers are screaming the command: *"Nicht Juden austreten!!! Nicht Juden austreten!!!"* (Non-Jews step forward!!!)

The Germans gather all the male Jews and make a *"Selektion!"* De-Nur is picked to dig a grave for another Jew who is to be humiliated and executed; the previous gravedigger was killed for not digging fast enough.

While under LSD in 1976, De-Nur recalls the 1939 grave-digging episode much differently, in particular, the talking worm:

From the earth the worm cries up to me: "I am life! I am life! Live!" it cries up to me. "Dig and stay alive! As long as your hands keep digging, you live!"[5]

Setting: *the place and conditions in which something happens or exists*

The place is Auschwitz and the message is from Daniel 5:26, 27. KZ is witness to the common butchery inside the death camp: "*Mene, mene tekel ... God hath numbered thy kingdom and finished it. Thou art weighed in the balances and art found wanting.*"

He's then back in the field digging the grave; then he's the Jew in the

---

[5] Ibid, 79.

field about to be executed; then is executed – only in his mind though. He sees the bullet pass through him and embrace the ground: *"I surrender my body to earth and my breath to my Creator, while an ineffable light fills me. I haven't known this light since my soul left the mansion of souls, an abode under the throne of Shekhina."*[6]

Science: *knowledge about or study of the natural world based on facts learned through experiments and observation*

KZ then shivers; his lightness of being is interrupted by a vow he made to the dead of Auschwitz ~ that he'd be their voice.

His bliss is checked by a particular memory: he sees the female S.S. German commander of the women's camp where his sister is held, and she's drunk, half-naked and coming at him.

---

[6] Ibid, 86; Shekhina is a divine presence in the Cabala.

His mind blocks the memory (for this session) and takes him back to the execution field; here he begins to bliss out again. He sees his soul soar in the vision of Neshama's flight ... and Dr. Bastiaans touches him.

De-Nur isn't so happy the doctor stopped the session: it was bliss after all.

The doctor agrees with him ... and notes that one can get lost there too.

GATE 5

"I see the Voice."

Set: *to fix as a distinguishing imprint, sign, or appearance*

This is the last session; De-Nur is able, in the fifth LSD-serotonin session with Dr. Bastiaans, to see his Auschwitz nightmare – and unbury it:

"What do you see, my Witness?"[7]

Setting: *the place and conditions in which something happens or exists*

He's in Auschwitz and the female S.S. Commander of the women prisoners approaches KZ pleading

---

[7] Ibid, 99.

with Siegfried (an S.S. officer) not to kill KZ. Siegfried instead takes KZ to see what they had done to his sister.

This is what Mr. De-Nur had been unable to see/recall prior to the LSD-serotonin therapy. By the fifth session, the medicine had journeyed with him through his memories and nightmares. He could now see his sister and what they did to her, as well as a vision of souls.

Even after all Mr. De-Nur witnessed at Auschwitz, he still had a spot he was protecting: a memory of his sister. That seems to have been it; the horror is no less brutal than the honor of his journey. To give witness to that and heal, it doesn't seem possible, yet that's what he did. Dr. Bastiaans recommended two more sessions: De-Nur declined. He'd found what he was searching for, he said, and wanted to go home, home to Israel.

Science: *knowledge about or study of the natural world based on facts learned through experiments and observation*

Mr. De-Nur came to see Professor Bastiaans after 30 years of Auschwitz nightmares. In five LSD-serotonin therapy sessions he found his answer locked in his mind.

In science terms, Mr. De-Nur's journey is called an "N of 1." His is definitely unique. He reports seeing the Voice, the Voice of God.

Dr. Bastiaans treated many others with LSD-serotonin therapy, and they too found success: so the N is more than 1.

GATE NIXON

*"No Jews. We are adamant when I say
no Jews."*
Nixon, 14 June 1973

Set: *to fix as a distinguishing imprint, sign,
or appearance*

Who is President Nixon referring to
when he says "We"? It's supposed
to have been the we of *We the
People*, and in essence it was; not
approving of course, just ... we did
create him.

Nixon's drug war makes a citizen an
Other, like an aborigine or Jew, and
then "things" can be done to
"them."

What we created, we can also end.

Setting: *the place and conditions in which something happens or exists*

Richard Wagner was the anti-Semitic European artist par excellence; Friedrich Nietzsche broke with him over it. For example, take in Nietzsche's *Daybreak (The Dawn): Thoughts on the prejudices of morality (1881)* for a human, all too human vision of Otherness: *"My rights are that part of my power which others have not only conceded to me but which they wish me to preserve."*

KZ 135633's Shivitti: A Vision is testimony to the healing nature of our bodies, clearly summed in a serotonergic Neshama flight.

Science: *knowledge about or study of the natural world based on facts learned through experiments and observation*

Nixon's law, the Controlled Substances Act of 1970, is not a law of We the People represented according to our Numbers.

Madison's way, the way of Enumerated Representation, is America's constitutional blueprint: we are to build America a new home, founded on the ratio *"thirty Thousand,"* a House where We the People, the Others, are legally counted and represented. A home for We the People is an American birthright.

Acknowledgements

Hannah Arendt

Albert Hoffman

Martin A. Lee & Bruce Shlain
   Acid Dreams (1985)

William Abens

Stephen R. Young

William D. Brickner

Janet E. (Hammer) Brickner

KZ 135633